The Poetry of Algernon Charles Swinburne

VOLUME IX – THE HEPTALOGIA or THE SEVEN AGAINST SENSE; A CAP WITH SEVEN BELLS

Algernon Charles Swinburne was born on April 5th, 1837, in London, into a wealthy Northumbrian family. He was educated at Eton and at Balliol College, Oxford, but did not complete a degree.

In 1860 Swinburne published two verse dramas but achieved his first literary success in 1865 with Atalanta in Calydon, written in the form of classical Greek tragedy. The following year "Poems and Ballads" brought him instant notoriety. He was now identified with "indecent" themes and the precept of art for art's sake.

Although he produced much after this success in general his popularity and critical reputation declined. The most important qualities of Swinburne's work are an intense lyricism, his intricately extended and evocative imagery, metrical virtuosity, rich use of assonance and alliteration, and bold, complex rhythms.

Swinburne's physical appearance was small, frail, and plagued by several other oddities of physique and temperament. Throughout the 1860s and 1870s he drank excessively and was prone to accidents that often left him bruised, bloody, or unconscious. Until his forties he suffered intermittent physical collapses that necessitated removal to his parents' home while he recovered.

Throughout his career Swinburne also published literary criticism of great worth. His deep knowledge of world literatures contributed to a critical style rich in quotation, allusion, and comparison. He is particularly noted for discerning studies of Elizabethan dramatists and of many English and French poets and novelists. As well he was a noted essayist and wrote two novels.

In 1879, Swinburne's friend and literary agent, Theodore Watts-Dunton, intervened during a time when Swinburne was dangerously ill. Watts-Dunton isolated Swinburne at a suburban home in Putney and gradually weaned him from alcohol, former companions and many other habits as well.

Much of his poetry in this period may be inferior but some individual poems are exceptional; "By the North Sea," "Evening on the Broads," "A Nympholept," "The Lake of Gaube," and "Neap-Tide."

Swinburne lived another thirty years with Watts-Dunton. He denied Swinburne's friends access to him, controlled the poet's money, and restricted his activities. It is often quoted that 'he saved the man but killed the poet'.

Swinburne died on April 10th, 1909 at the age of seventy-two.

Index of Contents

THE HIGHER PANTHEISM IN A NUTSHELL

One, who is not, we see: but one, whom we see not, is:
Surely this is not that: but that is assuredly this.

What, and wherefore, and whence? for under is over and under:
If thunder could be without lightning, lightning could be without thunder.

Doubt is faith in the main: but faith, on the whole, is doubt:
We cannot believe by proof: but could we believe without?

Why, and whither, and how? for barley and rye are not clover:
Neither are straight lines curves: yet over is under and over.

Two and two may be four: but four and four are not eight:
Fate and God may be twain: but God is the same thing as fate.

Ask a man what he thinks, and get from a man what he feels:
God, once caught in the fact, shows you a fair pair of heels.

Body and spirit are twins: God only knows which is which:
The soul squats down in the flesh, like a tinker drunk in a ditch.

More is the whole than a part: but half is more than the whole:
Clearly, the soul is the body: but is not the body the soul?

One and two are not one: but one and nothing is two:
Truth can hardly be false, if falsehood cannot be true.

Once the mastodon was: pterodactyls were common as cocks:
Then the mammoth was God: now is He a prize ox.

Parallels all things are: yet many of these are askew:
You are certainly I: but certainly I am not you.

Springs the rock from the plain, shoots the stream from the rock:
Cocks exist for the hen: but hens exist for the cock.

God, whom we see not, is: and God, who is not, we see:

Fiddle, we know, is diddle: and diddle, we take it, is dee.

I

AT THE PIANO

I

Love me and leave me; what love bids retrieve me? can June's fist grasp May?
Leave me and love me; hopes eyed once above me like spring's sprouts decay;
Fall as the snow falls, when summer leaves grow false—cards packed for storm's play!

II

Nay, say Decay's self be but last May's elf, wing shifted, eye sheathed—
Changeling in April's crib rocked, who lets 'scape rills locked fast since frost breathed—
Skin cast (think!) adder-like, now bloom bursts bladder-like,—bloom frost bequeathed?

III

Ah, how can fear sit and hear as love hears it grief's heart's cracked grate's screech?
Chance lets the gate sway that opens on hate's way and shews on shame's beach
Crouched like an imp sly change watch sweet love's shrimps lie, a toothful in each.

IV

Time feels his tooth slip on husks wet from Truth's lip, which drops them and grins—
Shells where no throb stirs of life left in lobsters since joy thrilled their fins—
Hues of the prawn's tail or comb that makes dawn stale, so red for our sins!

V

Years blind and deaf use the soul's joys as refuse, heart's peace as manure,
Reared whence, next June's rose shall bloom where our moons rose last year, just as pure:
Moons' ends match roses' ends: men by beasts' noses' ends mete sin's stink's cure.

VI

Leaves love last year smelt now feel dead love's tears melt—flies caught in time's mesh!
Salt are the dews in which new time breeds new sin, brews blood and stews flesh;

Next year may see dead more germs than this weeded and reared them afresh.

Old times left perish, there's new time to cherish; life just shifts its tune;
As, when the day dies, earth, half afraid, eyes the growth of the moon;
Love me and save me, take me or waive me; death takes one so soon!

II

BY THE CLIFF

I

Is it daytime (guess),
You that feed my soul
To excess
With that light in those eyes
And those curls drawn like a scroll
In that round grave guise?
No or yes?

II

Oh, the end, I'd say!
Such a foolish thing
(Pure girls' play!)
As a mere mute heart,
Was it worth a kiss, a ring,
This? for two must part—
Not to-day.

III

Look, the whole sand crawls,
Hums, a heaving hive,
Scrapes and scrawls—
Such a buzz and burst!
Here just one thing's not alive,
One that was at first—
But life palls.

IV

Yes, my heart, I know,
Just my heart's stone dead—
Yes, just so.
Sick with heat, those worms
Drop down scorched and overfed—
No more need of germs!
Let them go.

V

Yes, but you now, look,
You, the rouged stage female
With a crook,
Chalked Arcadian sham,
You that made my soul's sleep's dream ail—
Your soul fit to damn?
Shut the book.

III

ON THE SANDS

I

There was nothing at all in the case (conceive)
But love; being love, it was not (understand)
Such a thing as the years let fall (believe)
Like the rope's coil dropt from a fisherman's hand
When the boat's hauled up—"by your leave!"

II

So—well! How that crab writhes—leg after leg
Drawn, as a worm draws ring upon ring
Gradually, not gladly! Chicken or egg,
Is it more than the ransom (say) of a king
(Take my meaning at least) that I beg?

III

Not so! You were ready to learn, I think,

What the world said! "He loves you too well (suppose)
For such leanings! These poets, their love's mere ink—
Like a flower, their flame flashes—a rosebud, blows—
Then it all drops down at a wink!

IV

"Ah, the instance! A curl of a blossomless vine
The vinedresser passing it sickens to see
And mutters 'Much hope (under God) of His wine
From the branch and the bark of a barren tree
Spring reared not, and winter lets pine—

V

"'His wine that should glorify (saith He) the cup
That a man beholding (not tasting) might say
"Pour out life at a draught, drain it dry, drink it up,
Give this one thing, and huddle the rest away—
Save the bitch, and be hanged to the pup!"

VI

"'Let it rot then!' which saying, he leaves it—we'll guess,
Feels (if the sap move at all) thus much—
Yearns, and would blossom, would quicken no less,
Bud at an eye's glance, flower at a touch—
'Die, perhaps, would you not, for her?'—'Yes!'

VII

"Note the hitch there! That's piteous—so much being done,
(He'll think some day, your lover) so little to do!
Such infinite days to wear out, once begun!
Since the hand its glove holds, and the footsole its shoe—
Overhead too there's always the sun!"

VIII

Oh, no doubt they had said so, your friends—been profuse
Of good counsel, wise hints—"where the trap lurks, walk warily—
Squeeze the fruit to the core ere you count on the juice!
For the graft may fail, shift, wax, change colour, wane, vary, lie—"

You were cautious, God knows—to what use?

IX

This crab's wiser, it strikes me—no twist but implies life—
Not a curl but's so fit you could find none fitter—
For the brute from its brutehood looks up thus and eyes life—
Stoop your soul down and listen, you'll hear it twitter,
Laughing lightly,—my crab's life's the wise life!

X

Those who've read S. T. Coleridge remember how Sammy sighs
To his pensive (I think he says) Sara—"most soothing-sweet"—
Crab's bulk's less (look!) than man's—yet (quoth Cancer) I am my size,
And my bulk's girth contents me! Man's maw (see?) craves two things—wheat
And flesh likewise—man's gluttonous—damn his eyes!

XI

Crab's content with crab's provender: crab's love, if soothing,
Is no sweeter than pincers are soft—and a new sickle
Cuts no sharper than crab's claws nip, keen as boar's toothing!
Yet crab's love's no less fervent than bard's, if less musical—
'Tis a new thing I'd lilt—but a true thing.

XII

Old songs tell us, of all drinks for Englishmen fighting, ale's
Out and out best: salt water contents crab, it seems to me,
Though pugnacious as sailors, and skilled to steer right in gales
That craze pilots, if slow to sing—"Sleep'st thou? thou dream'st o' me!"
In such love-strains as mine—or a nightingale's.

XIII

Ah, now, look you—tail foremost, the beast sets seaward—
The sea draws it, sand sucks it—he's wise, my crab!
From the napkin out jumps his one talent—good steward,
Just judge! So a man shirks the smile or the stab,
And sets his sail duly to leeward!

XIV

Trust me? Hardly! I bid you not lean (remark)
On my spirit, your spirit—my flesh, your flesh—
Hold my hand, and tread safe through the horrible dark—
Quench my soul as with sprinklings of snow, then refresh
With some blast of new bellows the spark!

XV

By no means! This were easy (men tell me) to say—
"Give her all, throw your chance up, fall back on her heart!"
(Say my friends) "she must change! after night follows day—"
No such fool! I am safe set in hell, for my part—
So let heaven do the worst now he may!

XVI

What they bid me? Well, this, nothing more—"Tell her this—
'You are mine, I yours, though the whole world fail—
Though things are not, I know there is one thing which is—
Though the oars break, there's hope for us yet—hoist the sail!
Oh, your heart! what's the heart? but your kiss!'

XVII

"Then she breaks, she drops down, she lies flat at your feet—
Take her then!" Well, I knew it—what fools are men!
Take the bee by her horns, will your honey prove sweet?
Sweet is grass—will you pasture your cows in a fen?
Oh, if contraries could but once meet!

XVIII

Love you call it? Some twitch in the moon's face (observe),
Wet blink of her eyelid, tear dropt about dewfall,
Cheek flushed or obscured—does it make the sky swerve?
Fetch the test, work the question to rags, bring to proof all—
Find what souls want and bodies deserve!

XIX

Ah, we know you! Your soul works to infinite ends,

Frets, uses life up for death's sake, takes pains,
Flings down love's self—"but you, bear me witness, my friends!
Have I lost spring? count up (see) the winter's fresh gains!
Is the shrub spoilt? the pine's hair impends!"

XX

What, you'd say—"Mark how God works! Years crowd, time wears thin,
Earth keeps good yet, the sun goes on, stars hold their own,
And you'll change, climb past sight of the world, shift your skin,
Never heeding how life moans—'more flesh now, less bone!'
For that cheek's worn waste outline (death's grin)

XXI

"Pleads with time still—'what good if I lose this? but see—'"
(There's the crab gone!) "'I said, "Though earth sinks,"'" (you perceive?
Ah, true, back there!) your soul now—"'"yet some vein might be
(Could one find it alive in the heart's core's pulse, cleave
Through the life-springs where "you" melts in "me")—

XXII

"'"Some true vein of the absolute soul, which survives
All that flesh runs to waste through"—and lo, this fails!
Here's death close on us! One life? a million of lives!
Why choose one sail to watch of these infinite sails?
Time's a tennis-play? thank you, no, fives!

XXIII

"'Stop life's ball then!' Such folly! melt earth down for that,
Till the pure ore eludes you and leaves you raw scoriæ?
Pish, the vein's wrong!" But you, friends—come, what were you at
When God spat you out suddenly? what was the story He
Cut short thus, the growth He laid flat?

XXIV

Wait! the crab's twice alive, mark! Oh, worthy, your soul,
Of strange ends, great results, novel labours! Take note,
I reject this for one! (ay, now, straight to the hole!
Safe in sand there—your skirts smooth out all as they float!)

I, shirk drinking through flaws in the bowl?

XXV

Or suppose now that rock's cleft—grim, scored to the quick,
As a man's face kept fighting all life through gets scored,
Mossed and marked with grey purulent leprosies, sick,
Flat and foul as man's life here (be swift with your sword—
Cut the soul out, stuck fast where thorns prick!)

XXVI

—Say it let the rock's heart out, its meaning, the thing
All was made for, devised, ruled out gradually, planned—
Ah, that sea-shell, perhaps—since it lies, such a ring
Of pure colour, a cup full of sunbeams, to stand
(Say, in Lent) at the priest's hand—(no king!)

XXVII

Blame the cleft then? Praise rather! So—just a chance gone!
Had you said—"Save the seed and secure souls in flower"—
Ah, how time laughs, years palpitate, pro grapples con,
Till one day you shrug shoulders—"Well, gone, the good hour!"
Till one night—"Is God off now? or on?"

IV

UP THE SPOUT

I

Hi! Just you drop that! Stop, I say!
Shirk work, think slink off, twist friend's wrist?
Where that spined sand's lined band's the bay—
Lined blind with true sea's blue, as due—
Promising—not to pay?

II

For the sea's debt leaves wet the sand;
Burst worst fate's weights in one burst gun?

A man's own yacht, blown—What? off land?
Tack back, or veer round here, then—queer!
Reef points, though—understand?

III

I'm blest if I do. Sigh? be blowed!
Love's doves make break life's ropes, eh? Tropes!
Faith's brig, baulked, sides caulked, rides at road;
Hope's gropes befogged, storm-dogged and bogged—
Clogged, water-logged, her load!

IV

Stowed, by Jove, right and tight, away!
No show now how best plough sea's brow,
Wrinkling—breeze quick, tease thick, ere day,
Clear sheer wave's sheen of green, I mean,
With twinkling wrinkles—eh?

V

Sea sprinkles winkles, tinkles light
Shells' bells—boy's joys that hap to snap!
It's just sea's fun, breeze done, to spite
God's rods that scourge her surge, I'd urge—
Not proper, is it—quite?

VI

See, fore and aft, life's craft undone!
Crank plank, split spritsail—mark, sea's lark!
That grey cold sea's old sprees, begun
When men lay dark i' the ark, no spark,
All water—just God's fun!

VII

Not bright, at best, his jest to these
Seemed—screamed, shrieked, wreaked on kin for sin!
When for mirth's yell earth's knell seemed please
Some dumb new grim great whim in him
Made Jews take chalk for cheese.

Could God's rods bruise God's Jews? Their jowls
Bobbed, sobbed, gaped, aped the plaice in face:
None heard, 'tis odds, his—God's—folk's howls.
Now, how must I apply, to try
This hookiest-beaked of owls?

Well, I suppose God knows—I don't.
Time's crimes mark dark men's types, in stripes
Broad as fen's lands men's hands were wont
Leave grieve unploughed, though proud and loud
With birds' words—No! he won't!

One never should think good impossible.
Eh? say I'd hide this Jew's oil's cruse—
His shop might hold bright gold, engrossible
By spy—spring's air takes there no care
To wave the heath-flower's glossy bell!

But gold bells chime in time there, coined—
Gold! Old Sphinx winks there—"Read my screed!"
Doctrine Jews learn, use, burn for, joined
(Through new craft's stealth) with health and wealth—
At once all three purloined!

I rose with dawn, to pawn, no doubt,
(Miss this chance, glance untried aside?)
John's shirt, my—no! Ay, so—the lout!
Let yet the door gape, store on floor
And not a soul about?

Such men lay traps, perhaps—and I'm
Weak—meek—mild—child of woe, you know!
But theft, I doubt, my lout calls crime.
Shrink? Think! Love's dawn in pawn—you spawn
Of Jewry! Just in time!

V

OFF THE PIER

I

One last glance at these sands and stones!
Time goes past men, and lives to his liking,
Steals, and ruins, and sometimes atones.
Why should he be king, though, and why not I king?
There now, that wind, like a swarm of sick drones!

II

Is it heaven or mere earth (come!) that moves so and moans?
Oh, I knew, when you loved me, my soul was in flowerage—
Now the frost comes; from prime, though, I watched through to nones,
Read love's litanies over—his age was not our age!
No more flutes in this world for me now, dear! trombones.

III

All that youth once denied and made mouths at, age owns.
Facts put fangs out and bite us; life stings and grows viperous;
And time's fugues are a hubbub of meaningless tones.
Once we followed the piper; now why not the piper us?
Love, grown grey, plays mere solos; we want antiphones.

IV

And we sharpen our wits up with passions for hones,
Melt down loadstars for magnets, use women for whetstones,
Learn to bear with dead calms by remembering cyclones,
Snap strings short with sharp thumbnails, till silence begets tones,
Burn our souls out, shift spirits, turn skins and change zones;

V

Then the heart, when all's done with, wakes, whimpers, intones
Some lost fragment of tune it thought sweet ere it grew sick;
(Is it life that disclaims this, or death that disowns?)
Mere dead metal, scrawled bars—ah, one touch, you make music!
Love's worth saving, youth doubts, but experience depones.

VI

In the darkness (right Dickens) of Tom-All-Alone's
Or the Morgue out in Paris, where tragedy centuples
Life's effects by Death's algebra, Shakespeare (Malone's)
Might have said sleep was murdered—new scholiasts have sent you pills
To purge text of him! Bread? give me—Scotticè—scones!

VII

Think, what use, when youth's saddle galls bay's back or roan's,
To seek chords on love's keys to strike, other than his chords?
There's an error joy winks at and grief half condones,
Or life's counterpoint grates the C major of discords—
'Tis man's choice 'twixt sluts rose-crowned and queens age dethrones.

VIII

I for instance might groan as a bag-pipe groans,
Give the flesh of my heart for sharp sorrows to flagellate,
Grief might grind my cheeks down, age make sticks of my bones,
(Though a queen drowned in tears must be worth more than Madge elate)
Rose might turn burdock, and pine-apples cones;

IX

My skin might change to a pitiful crone's,
My lips to a lizard's, my hair to weed,
My features, in fact, to a series of loans;
Thus much is conceded; now, you, concede
You would hardly salute me by choice, John Jones?

THE POET AND THE WOODLOUSE

Said a poet to a woodlouse—"Thou art certainly my brother;
I discern in thee the markings of the fingers of the Whole;
And I recognize, in spite of all the terrene smut and smother,
In the colours shaded off thee, the suggestions of a soul.

"Yea," the poet said, "I smell thee by some passive divination,
I am satisfied with insight of the measure of thine house;
What had happened I conjecture, in a blank and rhythmic passion,
Had the æons thought of making thee a man, and me a louse.

"The broad lives of upper planets, their absorption and digestion,
Food and famine, health and sickness, I can scrutinize and test;
Through a shiver of the senses comes a resonance of question,
And by proof of balanced answer I decide that I am best."

"Man, the fleshly marvel, alway feels a certain kind of awe stick
To the skirts of contemplation, cramped with nympholeptic weight:
Feels his faint sense charred and branded by the touch of solar caustic,
On the forehead of his spirit feels the footprint of a Fate."

"Notwithstanding which, O poet," spake the woodlouse, very blandly,
"I am likewise the created,—I the equipoise of thee;
I the particle, the atom, I behold on either hand lie
The inane of measured ages that were embryos of me.

"I am fed with intimations, I am clothed with consequences,
And the air I breathe is coloured with apocalyptic blush:
Ripest-budded odours blossom out of dim chaotic stenches,
And the Soul plants spirit-lilies in sick leagues of human slush.

"I am thrilled half cosmically through by cryptophantic surgings,
Till the rhythmic hills roar silent through a spongious kind of blee:
And earth's soul yawns disembowelled of her pancreatic organs,
Like a madrepore if mesmerized, in rapt catalepsy.

"And I sacrifice, a Levite—and I palpitate, a poet;—
Can I close dead ears against the rush and resonance of things?
Symbols in me breathe and flicker up the heights of the heroic;
Earth's worst spawn, you said, and cursed me? look! approve me! I have wings.

"Ah, men's poets! men's conventions crust you round and swathe you mist-like,
And the world's wheels grind your spirits down the dust ye overtrod:
We stand sinlessly stark-naked in effulgence of the Christlight,
And our polecat chokes not cherubs; and our skunk smells sweet to God.

"For He grasps the pale Created by some thousand vital handles,
Till a Godshine, bluely winnowed through the sieve of thunderstorms,

Shimmers up the non-existent round the churning feet of angels;
And the atoms of that glory may be seraphs, being worms.

"Friends, your nature underlies us and your pulses overplay us;
Ye, with social sores unbandaged, can ye sing right and steer wrong?
For the transient cosmic, rooted in imperishable chaos,
Must be kneaded into drastics as material for a song.

"Eyes once purged from homebred vapours through humanitarian passion
See that monochrome a despot through a democratic prism;
Hands that rip the soul up, reeking from divine evisceration,
Not with priestlike oil anoint him, but a stronger-smelling chrism.

"Pass, O poet, retransfigured! God, the psychometric rhapsode,
Fills with fiery rhythms the silence, stings the dark with stars that blink;
All eternities hang round him like an old man's clothes collapsèd,
While he makes his mundane music—AND HE WILL NOT STOP, I THINK."

THE PERSON OF THE HOUSE

THE ACCOMPANIMENTS

I. THE MONTHLY NURSE

The sickly airs had died of damp;
Through huddling leaves the holy chime
Flagged; I, expecting Mrs. Gamp,
Thought—"Will the woman come in time?"
Upstairs I knew the matron bed
Held her whose name confirms all joy
To me; and tremblingly I said,
"Ah! will it be a girl or boy?"
And, soothed, my fluttering doubts began
To sift the pleasantness of things;
Developing the unshapen man,
An eagle baffled of his wings;
Considering, next, how fair the state
And large the license that sublimes
A nineteenth-century female fate—

Sweet cause that thralls my liberal rhymes!
And Chastities and colder Shames,
Decorums mute and marvellous,
And fair Behaviour that reclaims
All fancies grown erroneous,
Moved round me musing, till my choice
Faltered. A female in a wig
Stood by me, and a drouthy voice
Announced her—Mrs. Betsy Prig.

II. THE CAUDLE

Sweet Love that sways the reeling years,
The crown and chief of certitudes,
For whose calm eyes and modest ears
Time writes the rule and text of prudes—
That, surpliced, stoops a nuptial head,
Nor chooses to live blindly free,
But, with all pulses quieted,
Plays tunes of domesticity—
That Love I sing of and have sung
And mean to sing till Death yawn sheer,
He rules the music of my tongue,
Stills it or quickens, there or here.
I say but this: as we went up
I heard the Monthly give a sniff
And "if the big dog makes the pup—"
She murmured—then repeated "if!"
The caudle on a slab was placed;
She snuffed it, snorting loud and long;
I fled—I would not stop to taste—
And dreamed all night of things gone wrong.

III. THE SENTENCES

I

Abortive Love is half a sin;
But Love's abortions dearer far
Than wheels without an axle-pin
Or life without a married star.

II

My rules are hard to understand

For him whom sensual rules depress;
A bandbox in a midwife's hand
May hold a costlier bridal dress.

III

"I like her not; in fact I loathe;
Bugs hath she brought from London beds."
Friend! wouldst thou rather bear their growth
Or have a baby with two heads?

IDYL CCCLXVI

THE KID

My spirit, in the doorway's pause,
Fluttered with fancies in my breast;
Obsequious to all decent laws,
I felt exceedingly distressed.
I knew it rude to enter there
With Mrs. V. in such a state;
And, 'neath a magisterial air,
Felt actually indelicate.
I knew the nurse began to grin;
I turned to greet my Love. Said she—
"Confound your modesty, come in!
—What shall we call the darling, V.?"
(There are so many charming names!
Girls'—Peg, Moll, Doll, Fan, Kate, Blanche, Bab:
Boys'—Mahershahal-hashbaz, James,
Luke, Nick, Dick, Mark, Aminadab.)

Lo, as the acorn to the oak,
As well-heads to the river's height,
As to the chicken the moist yolk,
As to high noon the day's first white—
Such is the baby to the man.
There, straddling one red arm and leg,
Lay my last work, in length a span,
Half hatched, and conscious of the egg.
A creditable child, I hoped;
And half a score of joys to be
Through sunny lengths of prospect sloped
Smooth to the bland futurity.
O, fate surpassing other dooms,

O, hope above all wrecks of time!
O, light that fills all vanquished glooms,
O, silent song o'ermastering rhyme!
I covered either little foot,
I drew the strings about its waist;
Pink as the unshell'd inner fruit,
But barely decent, hardly chaste,
Its nudity had startled me;
But when the petticoats were on,
"I know," I said; "its name shall be
Paul Cyril Athanasius John."
"Why," said my wife, "the child's a girl."
My brain swooned, sick with failing sense;
With all perception in a whirl,
How could I tell the difference?
"Nay," smiled the nurse, "the child's a boy."
And all my soul was soothed to hear
That so it was: then startled Joy
Mocked Sorrow with a doubtful tear.
And I was glad as one who sees
For sensual optics things unmeet:
As purity makes passion freeze,
So faith warns science off her beat.
Blessed are they that have not seen,
And yet, not seeing, have believed:
To walk by faith, as preached the Dean,
And not by sight, have I achieved.
Let love, that does not look, believe;
Let knowledge, that believes not, look:
Truth pins her trust on falsehood's sleeve,
While reason blunders by the book.
Then Mrs. Prig addressed me thus;
"Sir, if you'll be advised by me,
You'll leave the blessed babe to us;
It's my belief he wants his tea."

LAST WORDS OF A SEVENTH-RATE POET

Bill, I feel far from quite right—if not further: already the pill
Seems, if I may say so, to bubble inside me. A poet's heart, Bill,
Is a sort of a thing that is made of the tenderest young bloom on a fruit.
You may pass me the mixture at once, if you please—and I'll thank you to boot
For that poem—and then for the julep. This really is damnable stuff!
(Not the poem, of course.) Do you snivel, old friend? well, it's nasty enough,
But I think I can stand it—I think so—ay, Bill, and I could were it worse.
But I'll tell you a thing that I can't and I won't. 'Tis the old, old curse—

The gall of the gold-fruited Eden, the lure of the angels that fell.
'Tis the core of the fruit snake-spotted in the hush of the shadows of hell,
Where a lost man sits with his head drawn down, and a weight on his eyes.
You know what I mean, Bill—the tender and delicate mother of lies,
Woman, the devil's first cousin—no doubt by the female side.
The breath of her mouth still moves in my hair, and I know that she lied,
And I feel her, Bill, sir, inside me—she operates there like a drug.
Were it better to live like a beetle, to wear the cast clothes of a slug,
Be the louse in the locks of the hangman, the mote in the eye of the bat,
Than to live and believe in a woman, who must one day grow aged and fat?
You must see it's preposterous, Bill, sir. And yet, how the thought of it clings!
I have lived out my time—I have prigged lots of verse—I have kissed (ah, that stings!)
Lips that swore I had cribbed every line that I wrote on them—cribbed—honour bright!
Then I loathed her; but now I forgive her; perhaps after all she was right.
Yet I swear it was shameful—unwomanly, Bill, sir—to say that I fibbed.
Why, the poems were mine, for I bought them in print. Cribbed? of course they were cribbed.
Yet I wouldn't say, cribbed from the French—Lady Bathsheba thought it was vulgar—
But picked up on the banks of the Don, from the lips of a highly intelligent Bulgar.
I'm aware, Bill, that's out of all metre—I can't help it—I'm none of your sort
Who set metres, by Jove, above morals—not exactly. They don't go to Court—
As I mentioned one night to that cowslip-faced pet, Lady Rahab Redrabbit
(Whom the Marquis calls Drabby for short). Well, I say, if you want a thing, grab it—
That's what I did, at least, when I took that danseuse to a swell cabaret,
Where expense was no consideration. A poet, you see, now and then must be gay.
(I declined to give more, I remember, than fifty centeems to the waiter;
For I asked him if that was enough; and the jackanapes answered—Peut-être.
Ah, it isn't in you to draw up a menu such as ours was, though humble:
When I told Lady Shoreditch, she thought it a regular grand tout ensemble.)
She danced the heart out of my body—I can see in the glare of the lights,
I can see her again as I saw her that evening, in spangles and tights.
When I spoke to her first, her eye flashed so, I heard—as I fancied—the spark whiz
From her eyelid—I said so next day to that jealous old fool of a Marquis.
She reminded me, Bill, of a lovely volcano, whose entrails are lava—
Or (you know my penchant for original types) of the upas in Java.
In the curve of her sensitive nose was a singular species of dimple,
Where the flush was the mark of an angel's creased kiss—if it wasn't a pimple.
Now I'm none of your bashful John Bulls who don't know a pilau from a puggaree
Nor a chili, by George, from a chopstick. So, sir, I marched into her snuggery,
And proposed a light supper by way of a finish. I treated her, Bill,
To six entrées of ortolans, sprats, maraschino, and oysters. It made her quite ill.
Of which moment of sickness I took some advantage. I held her like this,
And availed myself, sir, of her sneezing, to shut up her lips with a kiss.
The waiters, I saw, were quite struck; and I felt, I may say, entre nous,
Like Don Juan, Lauzun, Almaviva, Lord Byron, and old Richelieu.
(You'll observe, Bill, that rhyme's quite Parisian; a Londoner, sir, would have cited old Q.
People tell me the French in my verses recalls that of Jeames or John Thomas: I
Must maintain it's as good as the average accent of British diplomacy.)
These are moments that thrill the whole spirit with spasms that excite and exalt.

I stood more than the peer of the great Casanova—you know—de Seingalt.
She was worth, sir, I say it without hesitation, two brace of her sisters.
Ah, why should all honey turn rhubarb—all cherries grow onions—all kisses leave blisters?
Oh, and why should I ask myself questions? I've heard such before—once or twice.
Ah, I can't understand it—but, O, I imagine it strikes me as nice.
There's a deity shapes us our ends, sir, rough-hew them, my boy, how we will—
As I stated myself in a poem I published last year, you know, Bill—
Where I mentioned that that was the question—to be, or, by Jove, not to be.
Ah, it's something—you'll think so hereafter—to wait on a poet like me.
Had I written no more than those verses on that Countess I used to call Pussy—
Yes, Minette or Manon—and—you'll hardly believe it—she said they were all out of Musset.
Now I don't say they weren't—but what then? and I don't say they were—I'll bet pounds against pennies on
The subject—I wish I may never die Laureate, if some of them weren't out of Tennyson.
And I think—I don't like to be certain, with Death, so to speak, by me, frowning—
But I think there were some—say a dozen, perhaps, or a score—out of Browning.
And—though God knows his poems are not (as all mine are, sir) perfumed with orris—
Or at least with patchouli—I wouldn't be sworn there were none out of Morris.
And it's possible—only the legend of Circe is quite an old yarn—old
As the hills—that I might have been thinking, perhaps, of a poem by Arnold
When I sang how Ulysses—Odysseus I mean—would have yearned to dishevel her
Bright hair with his kisses, and painted myself at her feet—a Strayed Reveller.
As for poets who go on a contrary tack to what I go and you go—
You remember my lyrics translated—like "sweet bully Bottom"—from Hugo?
Though I will say it's curious that simply on just that account there should be
Men so bold as to say that not one of my poems was written by me.
It would stir the political bile or the physical spleen of a drab or a Tory
To hear critics disputing my claim to Empedocles, Maud, and the Laboratory.
Yes, it's singular—nay, I can't think of a parallel (ain't it a high lark?
As that Countess would say)—there are few men believe it was I wrote the Ode to a Skylark.
And it often has given myself and Lord Albert no end of diversion
To hear fellows maintain to my face it was Wordsworth who wrote the Excursion,
When they know that whole reams of the verses recur in my authorized works
Here and there, up and down! Why, such readers are infidels—heretics—Turks.
And the pitiful critics who think in their paltry presumption to pay me a
Pretty compliment, pairing me off, sir, with Keats—as if he could write Lamia!
While I never produced a more characteristic and exquisite book,
One that gave me more real satisfaction, than did, on the whole, Lalla Rookh.
Was it there that I called on all debtors, being pestered myself by a creditor, (he
Isn't paid yet) to rise, by the proud appellation of bondsmen—hereditary?
Yes—I think so. And yet, on my word, I can't think why I think it was so.
It more probably was in the poem I made a few seasons ago
On that Duchess—her name now? ah, thus one outlives a whole cycle of joys!
Fair supplants black and brown succeeds golden. The poem made rather a noise.
And indeed I have seen worse verses; but as for the woman, my friend—
Though his neck had been never so stiff, she'd have made a philosopher bend.
As the broken heart of a sunset that bleeds pure purple and gold
In the shudder and swoon of the sickness of colour, the agonies old

That engirdle the brows of the day when he sinks with a spasm into rest
And the splash of his kingly blood is dashed on the skirts of the west,
Even such was my own, when I felt how much sharper than any snake's tooth
Was the passion that made me mistake Lady Eve for her niece Lady Ruth.
The whole world, colourless, lapsed. Earth fled from my feet like a dream,
And the whirl of the walls of Space was about me, and moved as a stream
Flowing and ebbing and flowing all night to a weary tune
("Such as that of my verses"? Get out!) in the face of a sick-souled moon.
The keen stars kindled and faded and fled, and the wind in my ears
Was the wail of a poet for failure—you needn't come snivelling tears
And spoiling the mixture, confound you, with dropping your tears into that!
I know I'm pathetic—I must be—and you soft-hearted and fat,
And I'm grateful of course for your kindness—there, don't come hugging me, now—
But because a fellow's pathetic, you needn't low like a cow.

I should like—on my soul, I should like—to remember—but somehow I can't—
If the lady whose love has reduced me to this was the niece or the aunt.
But whichever it was, I feel sure, when I published my lays of last year
(You remember their title—The Tramp—only seven-and-sixpence—not dear),
I sent her a copy (perhaps her tears fell on the title-page—yes—
I should like to imagine she wept)—and the Bride of Bulgaria (MS.)
I forwarded with it. The lyrics, no doubt, she found bitter—and sweet;
But the Bride she rejected, you know, with expressions I will not repeat.
Well—she did no more than all publishers did. Though my prospects were marred,
I can pity and pardon them. Blindness, mere blindness! And yet it was hard.
For a poet, Bill, is a blossom—a bird—a billow—a breeze—
A kind of creature that moves among men as a wind among trees.
And a bard who is also the pet of patricians and dowagers doubly can
Express his contempt for canaille in his fables where beasts are republican.
Yet with all my disdainful forgiveness for men so deficient in ton
I cannot but feel it was cruel—I cannot but think it was wrong.
I with the heat of my heart still burning against all bars
As the fire of the dawn, so to speak, in the blanched blank brows of the stars—
I with my tremulous lips made pale by musical breath—
I with the shade in my eyes that was left by the kisses of Death—
(For Death came near me in youth, and touched my face with his face,
And put in my lips the songs that belong to a desolate place—
Desolate truly, my heart and my lips, till her kiss filled them up!)
I with my soul like wine poured out with my flesh for the cup—
It was hard for me—it was hard—Bill, Bill, you great owl, was it not?
For the day creeps in like a Fate: and I think my grand passion is rot:
And I dreamily seem to perceive, by the light of a life's dream done,
The lotion at six, and the mixture at ten, and the draught before one.

Yes—I feel rather better. Man's life is a mull, at the best;
And the patent perturbator pills are like bullets of lead in my chest.
When a man's whole spirit is like the lost Pleiad, a blown-out star,
Is there comfort in Holloway, Bill? is there hope of salvation in Parr?

True, most things work to their end—and an end that the shroud overlaps.
Under lace, under silk, under gold, sir, the skirt of a winding-sheet
flaps—
Which explains, if you think of it, Bill, why I can't, though my soul thereon broodeth,
Quite make out if I loved Lady Tamar as much as I loved Lady Judith.
Yet her dress was of violet velvet, her hair was hyacinth-hued,
And her ankles—no matter. A face where the music of every mood
Was touched by the tremulous fingers of passionate feeling, and made
Strange melodies, scornful, but sweeter than strings whereon sorrow has played
To enrapture the hearing of mirth when his garland of blossom and green
Turns to lead on the anguished forehead—"you don't understand what I mean"?
Well, of course I knew you were stupid—you always were stupid at school—
Now don't say you weren't—but I'm hanged if I thought you were quite such a fool!
You don't see the point of all this? I was talking of sickness and death—
In that poem I made years ago, I said this—"Love, the flower-time whose breath
Smells sweet through a summer of kisses and perfumes an autumn of tears
Is sadder at root than a winter—its hopes heavy-hearted like fears.
Though I love your Grace more than I love little Letty, the maid of the mill,
Yet the heat of your lips when I kiss them" (you see we were intimate, Bill)
"And the beat of the delicate blood in your eyelids of azure and white
Leave the taste of the grave in my mouth and the shadow of death on my sight.
Fill the cup—twine the chaplet—come into the garden—get out of the house—
Drink to me with your eyes—there's a banquet behind, where worms only carouse!
As I said to sweet Katie, who lived by the brook on the land Philip farmed—
Worms shall graze where my kisses found pasture!" The Duchess, I may say, was charmed.
It was read to the Duke, and he cried like a child. If you'll give me a pill,
I'll go on till past midnight. That poem was said to be—Somebody's, Bill.
But you see you can always be sure of my hand as the mother that bore me
By the fact that I never write verse which has never been written before me.
Other poets—I blush for them, Bill—may adore and repudiate in turn a
Libitina, perhaps, or Pandemos; my Venus, you know, is Laverna.
Nay, that epic of mine which begins from foundations the Bible is built on—
"Of man's first disobedience"—I've heard it attributed, dammy, to Milton.
Well, it's lucky for them that it's not worth my while, as I may say, to break spears
With the hirelings, forsooth, of the press who assert that Othello was Shakespeare's.
When he that can run, sir, may read—if he borrows the book, or goes on tick—
In my poems the bit that describes how the Hellespont joins the Propontic.
There are men, I believe, who will tell you that Gray wrote the whole of The Bard—
Or that I didn't write half the Elegy, Bill, in a Country Churchyard.
When you know that my poem, The Poet, begins—"Ruin seize thee!" and ends
With recapitulations of horrors the poet invokes on his friends.
And I'll swear, if you look at the dirge on my relatives under the turf, you
Will perceive it winds up with some lines on myself—and begins with the curfew.
Now you'll grant it's more probable, Bill—as a man of the world, if you please—
That all these should have prigged from myself than that I should have prigged from all these.
I could cry when I think of it, friend, if such tears would comport with my dignity,
That the author of Christabel ever should smart from such vulgar malignity.
(You remember perhaps that was one of the first little things that I carolled

After finishing Marmion, the Princess, the Song of the Shirt, and Childe Harold.)
Oh, doubtless it always has been so—Ah, doubtless it always will be—
There are men who would say that myself is a different person from me.
Better the porridge of patience a poor man snuffs in his plate
Than the water of poisonous laurels distilled by the fingers of hate.

'Tis a dark-purple sort of a moonlighted kind of a midnight, I know;
You remember those verses I wrote on Irene, from Edgar A. Poe?
It was Lady Aholibah Levison, daughter of old Lord St. Giles,
Who inspired those delectable strains, and rewarded her bard with her smiles.
There are tasters who've sipped of Castalia, who don't look on my brew as the brew:
There are fools who can't think why the names of my heroines of title should always be Hebrew.
'Twas my comrade, Sir Alister Knox, said, "Noo, dinna ye fash wi' Apollo, mon;
Gang to Jewry for wives and for concubines, lad—look at David and Solomon.
And it gives an erotico-scriptural twang," said that high-born young man, "—tickles
The lug" (he meant ear) "of the reader—to throw in a touch of the Canticles."
So I versified half of The Preacher—it took me a week, working slowly. Bah!
You don't half know the sex, Bill—they like it. And what if her name was Aholibah?
I recited her charms, in conjunction with those of a girl at the café,
In a poem I published in collaboration with Templeton (Taffy).
There are prudes in a world full of envy—and some of them thought it too strong
To compare an earl's daughter by name with a girl at a French restaurant.
I regarded her, though, with the chivalrous eyes of a knight-errant on quest;
I may say I don't know that I ever felt prouder, old friend, of a conquest.
And when I've been made happy, I never have cared a brass farthing who knew it; I
Thank my stars I'm as free from mock-modesty, friend, as from vulgar fatuity.
I can't say if my spirit retains—for the subject appears to me misty—any tie
To such associations as Poesy weaves round the records of Christianity.
There are bards—I may be one myself—who delight in their skill to unlock a lip's
Rosy secrets by kisses and whispers of texts from the charming Apocalypse.
It was thus that I won, by such biblical pills of poetical manna,
From two elders—Sir Seth and Lord Isaac—the liking of Lady Susanna.
But I left her—a woman to me is no more than a match, sir, at tennis is—
When I heard she'd gone off with my valet, and burnt my rhymed version of Genesis.
You may see by my shortness of speech that my time's almost up: I perceive
That my new-fangled brevity strikes you: but don't—though the public will—grieve.
As it's sometimes my whim to be vulgar, it's sometimes my whim to be brief;
As when once I observed, after Heine, that "she was a harlot, and I" (which is true) "was a thief."
(Though you hardly should cite this particular line, by the way, as an instance of absolute brevity:
I'm aware, man, of that; so you needn't disgrace yourself, sir, by such grossly mistimed and impertinent levity.)
I don't like to break off, any more than you wish me to stop: but my fate is
Not to vent half a million such rhymes without blockheads exclaiming—

JAM SATIS.

Specimen from the speaker's original poems.

Come into the orchard, Anne,
For the dark owl, Night, has fled,
And Phosphor slumbers, as well as he can
With a daffodil sky for a bed:
And the musk of the roses perplexes a man,
And the pimpernel muddles his head.

SONNET FOR A PICTURE

That nose is out of drawing. With a gasp,
She pants upon the passionate lips that ache
With the red drain of her own mouth, and make
A monochord of colour. Like an asp,
One lithe lock wriggles in his rutilant grasp.
Her bosom is an oven of myrrh, to bake
Love's white warm shewbread to a browner cake.
The lock his fingers clench has burst its hasp.
The legs are absolutely abominable.
Ah! what keen overgust of wild-eyed woes
Flags in that bosom, flushes in that nose?
Nay! Death sets riddles for desire to spell,
Responsive. What red hem earth's passion sews,
But may be ravenously unripped in hell?

NEPHELIDIA

From the depth of the dreamy decline of the dawn through a notable nimbus of nebulous noonshine,
Pallid and pink as the palm of the flag-flower that flickers with fear of the flies as they float,
Are they looks of our lovers that lustrously lean from a marvel of mystic miraculous moonshine,
These that we feel in the blood of our blushes that thicken and threaten with throbs through the throat?
Thicken and thrill as a theatre thronged at appeal of an actor's appalled agitation,
Fainter with fear of the fires of the future than pale with the promise of pride in the past;
Flushed with the famishing fullness of fever that reddens with radiance of rathe recreation,
Gaunt as the ghastliest of glimpses that gleam through the gloom of the gloaming when ghosts go aghast?
Nay, for the nick of the tick of the time is a tremulous touch on the temples of terror,
Strained as the sinews yet strenuous with strife of the dead who is dumb as the dust-heaps of death:
Surely no soul is it, sweet as the spasm of erotic emotional exquisite error,
Bathed in the balms of beatified bliss, beatific itself by beatitude's breath.
Surely no spirit or sense of a soul that was soft to the spirit and soul of our senses
Sweetens the stress of suspiring suspicion that sobs in the semblance and sound of a sigh;
Only this oracle opens Olympian, in mystical moods and triangular tenses—
"Life is the lust of a lamp for the light that is dark till the dawn of the day when we die."
Mild is the mirk and monotonous music of memory, melodiously mute as it may be,

While the hope in the heart of a hero is bruised by the breach of men's rapiers, resigned to the rod;
Made meek as a mother whose bosom-beats bound with the bliss-bringing bulk of a balm-breathing baby,
As they grope through the grave-yard of creeds, under skies growing green at a groan for the grimness of God.
Blank is the book of his bounty beholden of old, and its binding is blacker than bluer:
Out of blue into black is the scheme of the skies, and their dews are the wine of the bloodshed of things;
Till the darkling desire of delight shall be free as a fawn that is freed from the fangs that pursue her,
Till the heart-beats of hell shall be hushed by a hymn from the hunt that has harried the kennel of kings.

Algernon Charles Swinburne – A Short Biography

Algernon Charles Swinburne was born at 7 Chester Street, Grosvenor Place, in London, on April 5th, 1837. He was the eldest of six children born to Captain Charles Henry Swinburne and Lady Jane Henrietta, daughter of the 3rd Earl of Ashburnham, a wealthy Northumbrian family.

Swinburne spent his early years at East Dene in Bonchurch, on the Isle of Wight. As a child, Swinburne was nervous and frail, but also imbued with a nervous energy and fearlessness almost to the point of recklessness.

He was schooled at Eton College from 1849 to 1853. It was here that he first began to write poetry. He excelled at languages and whilst still at Eton won first prizes in both French and Italian.

From Eton he moved to Oxford where he attended at Balliol College from 1856. Here he met friends to whom he became closely attached, among them Dante Gabriel Rossetti, William Morris and Edward Burne-Jones, who in 1857, were painting their Arthurian murals on the walls of the Oxford Union. At Oxford Swinburne was mentored by Benjamin Jowett, the master of Balliol College, who recognised his poetic talent and, intervening on his behalf, tried to keep him from being expelled when he celebrated the Italian patriot Orsini, and his failed attempt on the life of Napoleon III in 1858. Swinburne had to leave the Universcity for a few months due to this but returned in May, 1860 but never received a degree.

Summers were usually spent at Capheaton Hall in Northumberland, the house of his grandfather, Sir John Swinburne, 6th Baronet, who had a famous library and was himself President of the Literary and Philosophical Society in Newcastle upon Tyne.

Swinburne proudly considered himself a native of Northumberland and this is reflected in poems such as the intensely patriotic 'Northumberland' and 'Grace Darling'. He enjoyed riding across the moors and was, it was said, a daring horseman, as he moved 'through honeyed leagues of the northland border', as he remembered the Scottish border in his Recollections.

In the period from 1857 to 1860, Swinburne was one of a number of Pre-Raphaelite's who visited and became part of Lady Pauline Trevelyan's intellectual circle at Wallington Hall, a few miles west of Morpeth in Northumberland.

After leaving college, he moved to London and began his career in earnest as well as becoming a constant visitor to the Rossetti's house. To Rossetti Swinburne was his 'little Northumbrian friend', an affectionate reference to Swinburne's small stature—a mere five foot four. Whatever Swinburne lacked in height he made up for in poetic talent. However, with the burden of such great talent came the unveiling of a dark side that was to cause him pain and would, at times, threaten his very existence with all manner of self-inflicted pains through drink, drugs and sado-machoism.

In 1860 Swinburne published two verse dramas; The Queen Mother and Rosamond but it would not be until 1865 that Swinburne would achieve literary success with Atalanta in Calydon.

In 1861, Swinburne visited Menton on the French Riviera to recover from the effects of yet another period of excess use of alcohol, staying at the Villa Laurenti. From Menton, Swinburne then travelled on to Italy, where he journeyed widely.

After Elizabeth Rossetti's death from suicide in 1862, he and Rossetti moved to Tudor House at 16 Cheyne Walk in Chelsea. The stories that survive from his year with Rossetti are typical Swinburne. In one, Rossetti once had to tell him to keep down the noise — he and a boyfriend had been sliding naked down the bannisters and disturbing Rossetti's painting. He took a sardonic delight in what the critic and biographer, Cecil Lang, calls "Algernonic exaggeration": When people began to talk scathingly about his homosexuality and other sexual proclivities, he circulated a story that he had engaged in pederasty and bestiality with a monkey — and then eaten it. How many of the stories were true and how many invented is unclear. Oscar Wilde called him "a braggart in matters of vice, who had done everything he could to convince his fellow citizens of his homosexuality and bestiality without being in the slightest degree a homosexual or a bestialiser."

In December 1862, Swinburne accompanied Scott and his guests on a trip to Tynemouth. Scott writes in his memoirs that, as they walked by the sea, Swinburne declaimed the as yet unpublished 'Hymn to Proserpine' and 'Laus Veneris' in his lilting intonation, while the waves 'were running the whole length of the long level sands towards Cullercoats and sounding like far-off acclamations'.

Swinburne possessed a curious combination of frail health and strength. He was small and slightly built, but an excellent swimmer and the first to climb Culver Cliff on the Isle of Wight. He had an extremely excitable disposition: people who met him described him as a "demoniac boy" who would go skipping about the room declaiming poetry at the top of his voice. In this as in many things, moderation was not the standard for him. Excess was. Once or twice he had fits, thought to be epileptic, in public; but he made this condition much worse by drinking past excess to unconsciousness. More than once he was delivered to the door in the small of the night, dead drunk. Throughout the 1860s and '70s he rode an alcoholic cycle of dissolution, collapse, drying out at home in the country, then returning to London where he would begin the cycle all over again.

His mania for masochism, particularly flagellation, most probably started in early childhood at Eton and was encouraged by his later friendships with Richard Monckton Milnes (one of Tennyson's fellow Apostles), who introduced him to the works of the Marquis de Sade, and Richard Burton, the Victorian explorer and adventurer. Swinburne was an alcoholic and algolagniac (a desire for sexual gratification through inflicting pain on oneself or others; sadomasochism). He found life difficult, unfulfilling but still his poetic talents pushed to the fore.

Although Swinburne continued to publish some works in periodicals in 1865 he was granted recognition by both public and critics with Atalanta in Calydon written in the style of a classical Greek tragedy.

There followed "Laus Veneris" and Poems and Ballads (1866), with their sexually charged passages, absolutely decadent for polite Victorian society, which were attacked all the more violently as a result. The poems written in homage of Sappho of Lesbos such as "Anactoria" and "Sapphics" were especially savaged. The volume also contained poems such as "The Leper," "Laus Veneris," and "St Dorothy" which evoke both Swinburne's and a general Victorian fascination with the Middle Ages, and are explicitly mediaeval in style, tone and construction. With its publication came instant notoriety. He was now identified with indecent and decadent themes and the precept of art for art's sake.

Swinburne's meeting in 1867 with his long-time hero Mazzini, the Italian patriot living in England in exile, was the beginning of a poetical journey that now became more serious and more engaged with serious thought, initially leading to the political poems in the volume Songs Before Sunrise.

Also in 1867 he was introduced to Adah Isaacs Menken, the American actress, poet and circus rider, whose main fame seemed to be riding naked on a horse (in fact she wore tight nude coloured clothing) for her performance in the melodrama Mazeppa (itself based on a poem by Lord Byron). Although they had a short affair Adah's quote implies that Swinburne was not ready for a relationship that did not involve some self-sabotage; "I can't make him understand that biting's no use."

In 1879, with Swinburne nearly dead from alcoholism and dissolution, his legal advisor Theodore Watts-Dunton took him in, and was gradually successful in getting him to adapt to a healthier lifestyle. Swinburne lived the rest of his life at Watts-Dunton's house. He saw less and less of his old bohemian friends, who thought him a prisoner at The Pines, but his growing deafness also accounts for some of his decreased sociability. By now Swinburne was 42, and was moving from a young man of rebelliousness to a figure of social respectability. It was said of Watts-Dunton that he saved the man and killed the poet.

It is clear that Swinburne had an addictive personality, and clearly incapable of moderation in his pursuit of any chosen vices. This, of course, would both nourish and perhaps sabotage his poetic career. His poetry follows the somewhat clichéd pattern of early flourish and later decline; indeed some of the fresher pieces in the second and third series of Poems and Ballads (published in 1878 and 1889) were actually written during his days at Oxford. Nevertheless, his last collection, A Channel Passage, has some beautiful poems, including "The Lake of Gaube."

He is best remembered as the supreme technician in metre, with a versatility which exceeds even Tennyson's, but which lacks a corresponding emotional range. His obsessions are not widely enough shared; and if he cannot shock us by the strangeness of his desires nor the shrillness of his anti-theistical exclamations, often what remains is not enough to fully engage with the audience.

Swinburne is considered a poet of the decadent school, although he perhaps professed to more vice than he actually indulged in to advertise his deviance. Common gossip of the time reported that he also had a deep crush on the explorer Sir Richard Francis Burton, despite the fact that Swinburne himself abhorred travel. Fact and fiction are easily absorbed by the other so are difficult to untangle even now.

Many critics consider his mastery of vocabulary, rhyme and metre impressive, although he has also been criticised for his florid style and word choices that only fit the rhyme scheme rather than contributing to the meaning of the piece. A. E. Housman, although a critic, had great praise for his rhyming ability: to

Swinburne the sonnet was child's play: the task of providing four rhymes was not hard enough, and he wrote long poems in which each stanza required eight or ten rhymes, and wrote them so that he never seemed to be saying anything for the rhyme's sake.

Throughout his career Swinburne published literary criticism of great worth. His deep knowledge of world literatures contributed to a critical style rich in quotation, allusion, and comparison. He is particularly noted for discerning studies of Elizabethan dramatists and of many English and French poets and novelists. As well he was a noted essayist and wrote two novels.

Swinburne was nominated for the Nobel Prize in Literature every year from 1903 to 1907 and then again in 1909.

H.P. Lovecraft, the master of the dark side and a decent poet himself, considered Swinburne "the only real poet in either England or America after the death of Mr. Edgar Allan Poe."

Swinburne was also responsible for devising a poetic form called the roundel, a variation of the French Rondeau form. In 1883 he published A Century of Roundels with several of the roundels dedicated to Dante's sister, the poet Christina Georgina Rossetti. Swinburne wrote to Edward Burne-Jones in 1883: "I have got a tiny new book of songs or songlets, in one form and all manner of metres ... just coming out, of which Miss Rossetti has accepted the dedication. I hope you and Georgie [his wife Georgiana] will find something to like among a hundred poems of nine lines each, twenty-four of which are about babies or small children".

Opinions of the Roundel poems move between those who find them captivating and brilliant, to others who find them merely clever and contrived. One of them, A Baby's Death, was set to music by the English composer Sir Edward Elgar as the song "Roundel: The little eyes that never knew Light".

After the first Poems and Ballads, Swinburne's later poetry was devoted more to philosophy and politics, including the unification of Italy, particularly in the volume Songs before Sunrise. He did not stop writing love poetry entirely, indeed it was only in 1882 that his great epic-length poem, Tristram of Lyonesse, was published, its contents lyrical rather than shocking. His versification, and especially his rhyming technique, remain of high quality to the end.

Algernon Charles Swinburne died of influenza, at the Pines in London on April 10th, 1909 at the age of 72. He was buried at St. Boniface Church, Bonchurch on the Isle of Wight.

Algernon Charles Swinburne – A Concise Bibliography

Verse Drama
The Queen Mother (1860)
Rosamond (1860)
Chastelard (1865)
Bothwell (1874)
Mary Stuart (1881)
Marino Faliero (1885)
Locrine (1887)

The Sisters (1892)
Rosamund, Queen of the Lombards (1899)

*Although formally tragedies, Atlanta in Calydon and Erechtheus are traditionally included with his poetry.

www.ingramcontent.com/pod-product-compliance
Lightning Source LLC
Chambersburg PA
CBHW070113070426
42448CB00038B/2644